AF483083

First published in 2024

Written by Shawn and Hannah Macking
Book design by Bryony van der Merwe

ISBN: 979-8-218-41847-2 (hardcover)

BVI,
we never want to say goodbye
Shawn and Hannah Macking

We jump on the sailboat
with life jackets on.
We kick off our shoes
and hurry along.

Provisions of food
stowed safely away.
Now drop the lines,
and we're underway!

It's time to hoist sails,
another wrap on that winch.
Head into the wind;
the main's up in a pinch.

Our first stop is here;
the mooring ball is in sight.
Mom grabs the lines,
and we cleat them so tight.

It's Cooper Island,
where we play 'Shut the Box'.
Then it's back to our boat;
time to climb some rocks.

A quick sail to The Baths
has us swimming to shore.
These boulders are huge;
there's so much to explore!

Back at the boat,
we're happy and spent.
A quick nap while we sail
like Mom and Dad meant.

On our way to Bitter End,
we enter North Sound.
We radio ahead.
Where can our slip be found?

We jump off the boat,
ready to roam.
We see friendly faces;
we're finally home.

At BEYC, a regatta begins.
We sail hobies fast,
trying to win.

A dinghy ride takes us
out to Saba Rock.
Where we watch them
feed Tarpon right from the dock.

The drowned island is next, where time slows down.
Anegada's a favorite,
with the best beaches around.

Cannonballs and dives
off the side of the boat.
We love to swim
and splash and float.

We head to shore
and grab a taxi to cruise.
We see donkeys and cows
filling our views.

Cow Wreck is perfect;
there's no one in sight.
Ocean colors seem to change
with the light.

Back on the boat,
Mom and Dad cook dinner.
We play a game
and hope to be the winner.

Tummies are full,
and our jammies are on.
It's time for our favorite tradition, c'mon!

Cookies on the bow
while the sun sets!
We're not ready to go to sleep yet.

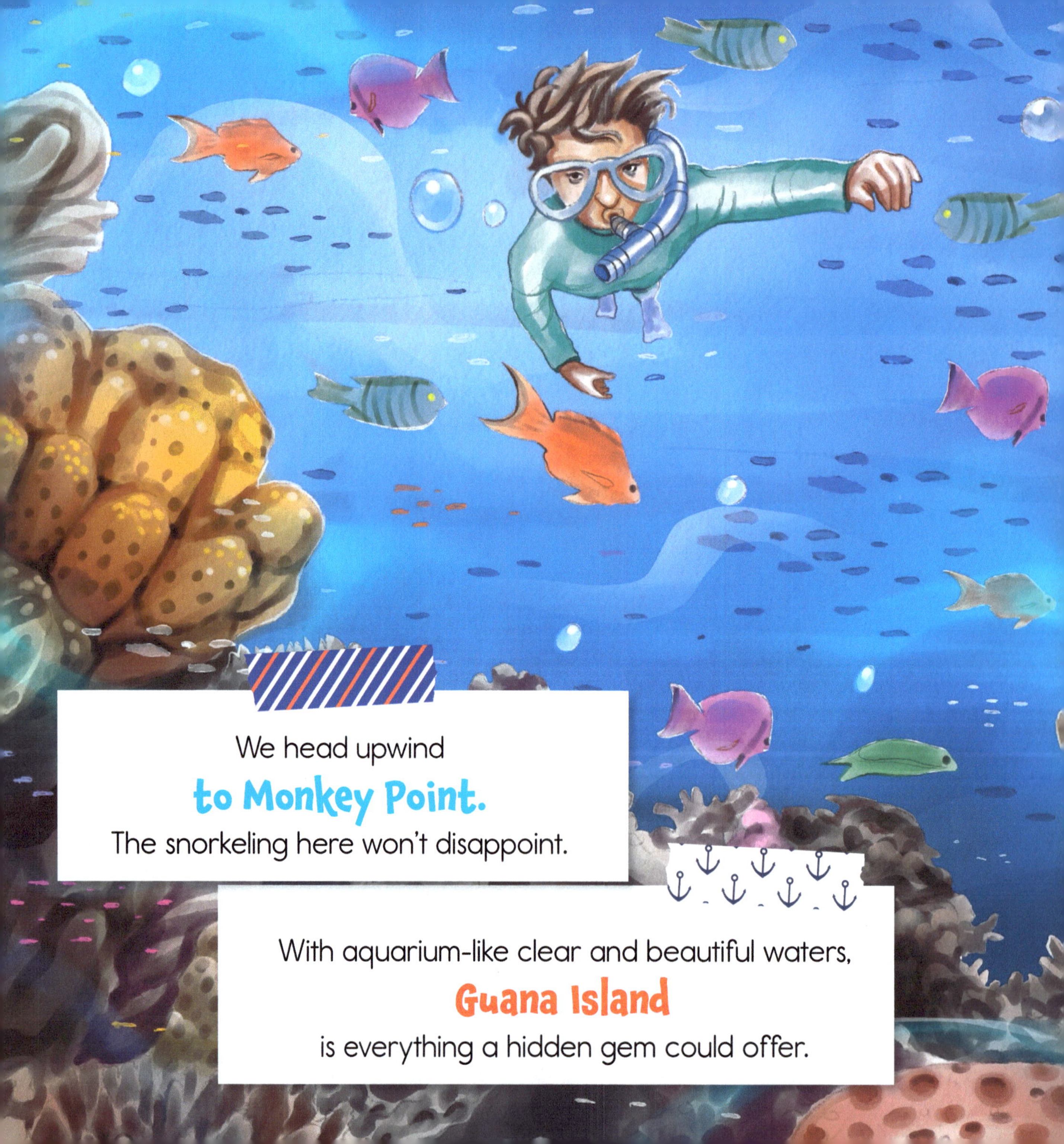

We head upwind
to Monkey Point.
The snorkeling here won't disappoint.

With aquarium-like clear and beautiful waters,
Guana Island
is everything a hidden gem could offer.

Next up, we head to
Jost Van Dyke,
a special island we really like.
Foxy's on the first night,
gets us feeling just right.
FOXY'S

Our first Virgin Painkiller **at Soggy Dollar.** Then, a quick dip in the cool turquoise water.

The last stop on our trip is
the Willy T.
We feel very happy, wild, and free.

Even though it's a really high drop,
we hold our breath
and jump off the top.

We have sailed and swum and played in the sand.
Bonded with family
and explored on land.

These islands are so perfect, it's hard to believe.
We can't wait to come back,
but we don't want to leave.

You were good to us, BVI.
It's so hard to say goodbye.

About the Authors

The Mackings are a family of four with a passion for sailing and traveling. Through their adventures in life, they hope to inspire other families to embrace the freedom of the sea and the wonders beyond the horizon.

You can follow their adventures on Instagram at @bareboatfamily.